HAPPY AS LARRY

FOR NUALA

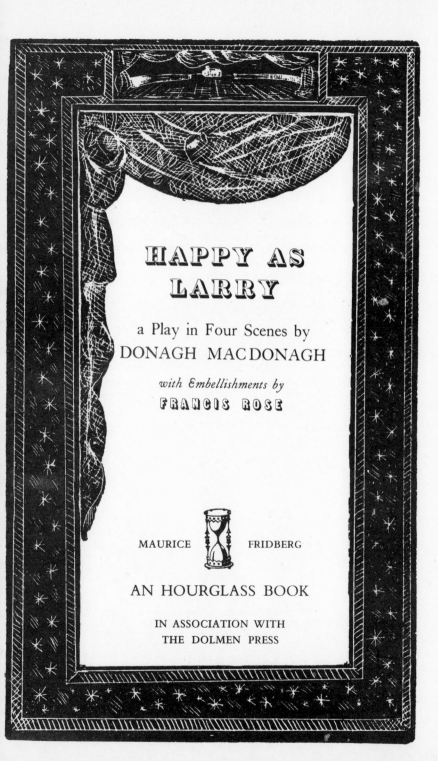

HAPPY AS LARRY

a Play in Four Scenes by
DONAGH MAC DONAGH

with Embellishments by
FRANCIS ROSE

MAURICE   FRIDBERG

AN HOURGLASS BOOK

IN ASSOCIATION WITH
THE DOLMEN PRESS

Set in twelve point Bembo and printed in the
Republic of Ireland by Hely Thom Ltd. for Maurice Fridberg

AN HOURGLASS BOOK
Published by Maurice Fridberg in association with
The Dolmen Press
8 Herbert Place, Dublin 2

First published 1946
New Edition 1967

*Distributed outside Ireland
except in the United States of America, and Canada
by Oxford University Press*

CHARACTERS:

LARRY: *Slick, slight, whimsical-looking, aged thirty-four, with a strong Dublin accent.*

MRS. LARRY: *A fine figure of a woman, aged thirty-two, her accent is not so strong and inclines rather to 'grandeur.'*

WIDOW: *A buxom, healthy girl of twenty, good-humoured and witty.*

DOCTOR: *Traditional villain, moustache and all. Very ponderous delivery. Aged about forty.*

SEAMUS: *The local pharmacist; a mean-looking type, deferential and of course untrustworthy. About forty.*

GRAVEDIGGER: *A very lugubrious individual dressed in the peculiar white garments in vogue in Glasnevin. Aged about fifty.*

TAILORS: *All speak with the accent of Dublin; they vary in age according to the actors available, but Number Five must be young and healthy. Their clothes are of no particular period, but suggest Irish country dress.*

NEIGHBOURS: *Silent but sympathetic.*

Note : There is a Glossary of hard words at the back.

SCENE I

The stage is divided longi-
tudinally by a curtain behind
which is the stage proper.
As the outer curtains are
opened six tailors are discovered, three on either side
of the stage.

IST TAILOR

Love is the proper food of man

2ND TAILOR

Woman curses every plan

3RD TAILOR

I married twice and would again

4TH TAILOR

I married once and there's my pain

5TH TAILOR

I could love all that pass the door

6TH TAILOR

My wife has never passed the door

IST TAILOR

I rhymed out poetry in my youth
To net the love I had for one;
But now that time has crossed my knees
I'd sooner slumber in the sun.

2ND TAILOR

I've never met the woman yet
I'd trust around the corner;
Give them leg-bail and they're gone
With hangman or informer.

3RD TAILOR

My grandpapa taught me the trick
To hold a woman's love—
Treat her decent and she'll snuggle
Like hand inside a glove.

8

4TH TAILOR

My wife would drink the Shannon dry
And after that the Barrow;
Do you wonder that my son
Has whiskey in his marrow?

5TH TAILOR

Each girl that passes by inclines
My mind to thoughts of fern and heather,
A haystack in an Autumn field
A bed of curling hair or feather;
Every blouse invites a glance,
Every mouth demands a kiss—
Here I stitch the world away
Who would be laying that by this.

6TH TAILOR

Marry son and you will find
Love's not cake, but bread and butter;
Lay your needle on the shelf
And out you go, into the gutter.

2ND TAILOR

My grandfather was married twice,
One wife was good and one was bad;
But which was bad and which was good
Was a puzzle always to my grandad.

5TH TAILOR

Tell us all about his marriage,
I'd talk of women till night cracked down,
Were his wives fair or were they black,
Were they red or were they brown?
Had they what would fill the hand,
Or was that flat which should be round?
Were they symmetrically planned,
With here a vale, and there a mound?

9

4TH TAILOR

Did they guzzle wine at night
And hide the bottle in a ditch?

5TH TAILOR

Or did they leave the curtains back
And stand at the window without a stitch?

3RD TAILOR

Were they modest wives and mothers,
Washing, scrubbing, cleaning, cooking?

6TH TAILOR

Dressed demurely, softly speaking?
Gently loving, and good-looking?

1ST TAILOR

Love is the proper food of man
And love talk must delight the mind,
So tell us friend how your grand-da
Disliked one wife and found one kind.

2ND TAILOR

My grandfather was married first
When he was nineteen years of age,
And she was great and he was small,
She the book and he the page;
For fifteen years they lived together
And it always was spring weather.

5TH TAILOR

So 'twill be when I am wed,
She the body, I the head.

2ND TAILOR

One day my grand-da took a walk
And past the outskirts of the town
Saw, kneeling by a recent grave,
A woman in a mourning gown.

[*The curtains of the inner stage are opened and the*
WIDOW *is discovered kneeling beside a grave and fanning
it while she chants. She is a buxom, healthy, handsome girl
of twenty who is doing her best to look mournful.*]

WIDOW

One for love and one for death
And one for every day of life;
One for every hour I've wept
And one for every faithful wife.

[*Enter* LARRY, *who stands looking at her. He is a slick,
slight, whimsical-looking man with a strong Dublin accent.*]

WIDOW

One for love and one for death
And one for every day of life;
One for every hour I've wept
And one for every faithful wife.
One for love and one for death . . .

[*She notices* LARRY *and falters, but continues softly to
herself as she fans the grave.*]

LARRY

I wonder what ails her at all
To be fanning the earth of a grave,
It's the queerest thing I've ever seen,
But I better step up and be brave
And question this queer looking act.
She's a gas looking widow all right
With her leg stripped up to the knee,
Though indeed it's a very nice sight.
    [*to* WIDOW]
What's your trouble, woman dear?
That's a doleful song I hear.

WIDOW

One for every hour I've wept
And one for every faithful wife.

LARRY

I was just passing by on the road
And I saw yourself here at your job,
And the first thought that popped in my head
Was that someone had come in to rob;
But as soon as I looked at yourself
And the eyes gone back in your head
I knew that you were no prowler
But one lamenting her dead.

WIDOW

One for love and one for death
And one for every hour of life . . .

LARRY

I've seen people beating their breast,
I've seen ould ones tearing their hair,
But fanning a grave is an act
That I've never seen anywhere.

WIDOW

One for every hour I've wept
And one for every faithful wife.

LARRY

Did you ever meet Michael Molloy
That was fighting in India a while?
Well, he says that when one of them dies
He's burnt to be buried in style;
Right up on the fire will go Jem,
Stretched out all ready to burn,
And the missus is hooshed up beside him
And the two of them cooked to a turn.

WIDOW

One for love and one for death
And one for every faithful wife.

LARRY

There's another I read of one time
Called Dido, a queen of some sort
Got caught in a jam with a sailor
Whose anchor was dropped in her port;
Well, of course Jem packed up one fine day,
Went home to the kids and the wife
Never saying a word to me lassie—
He set too much store by his life.
When me bold girl gets up in the morning
And hears the terrible news
She jumps up on top of a bonfire
And soon she's burned down to her shoes.

WIDOW

One for every hour I've wept
And one for every faithful wife.

LARRY

Fair enough; if you won't talk
I'd better continue with my walk.

WIDOW

Don't leave me. This is the second day I've spent
In this dirty, cold and miserable spot.

LARRY

I wouldn't say it was healthy at all,
Come down to the corner and have a ball
Of malt, or better come home with me
And the missus will make you a scald of tea.

WIDOW

And leave my work undone that any shower
May ruin in a quarter of an hour?

LARRY

Arrah, what work? If the Gardai caught you here
They'd get two doctors and certify you queer.

WIDOW

Would you have me break the promise that I
      made?

LARRY

Instead of 'Therefore' and 'Because'
Will you tell us what the promise was?

WIDOW

My Johnny died, the finest man you'd see
In two day's walk, a healthy, lusty man
That never saw a doctor in his life.

LARRY

I've a cousin a doctor in Merrion Square,
As decent a man as ever grew hair.

WIDOW

'Twas oysters that finished Johnny. Oysters and stout
Lobsters and prawns and shrimps, cockles and perry-
      winkles,
Crayfish and crabs with claws like garden shears,
Cockles and mussels, raw or cooked in milk;
All strange fish delighted him.
Gallons of stout he'd drink, then brown bread and butter
And raw eggs in the morning, downed with sherry.

LARRY

That was a fearsome galaxy of food,
In place of killing it should have done him good

WIDOW

And yet it killed him. Thursday Jack the Fish
Brought up three dozen oysters and a crab,
And Johnny, sitting in the blazing sun,
Opened the lot and downed them like a calf
Butting a can of milk. Before the night
Was out he was lying roaring in his bed
Shouting he'd died for love of me, and no R
In the month. Friday his nails turned blue,

His hair fell out. He called me over close
And caught my hands in his. "Promise," says he,
"That till the clay is dry over my grave
You'll never marry another. Promise," says he,
"That you'll remember Johnny that died for you."
And so I promised, though I still can't see
How stuffing shellfish down his throat was love!

LARRY

Lobsters are lecherous, they say,
And oysters amorous,
And even Hercules, that powerful man,
Found love laborious.

WIDOW

Those were before my time, but Johnny was
A fine, big, strong, hefty lump
Of a man, a kindly man, a very loving
Man, a man that slept but little in the night
And gave me little sleep, but would lie down
And slumber in the day in any ditch.

LARRY

So that's why you're making yourself a slave,
Because you promised to dry his grave?

WIDOW

He never mentioned a word like that, he said
Only I shouldn't marry till the earth
Was dry, and here I am two days at work
And maybe will have to work another week.

LARRY

Why break your heart with all this hurrying?
Is there another waiting with a ring?

WIDOW

Didn't I say I loved my husband well?
A finer, stronger man I never met,
And since the day that I was seventeen,
And that's a good three years, no man has ever
Touched me or kissed me, held me in the dark,
Tip-tapped with fingers under a table-cloth,
Whispered through door-crack, waited under
    windows.

I never loitered coming home from Mass.
My eyes behind drawn curtains kept their distance
And if the men that passed me in the street
Turned round to stare I never noticed them—
Stand out of the light there now, you'll shade the sun
Or keep the breeze from blowing on the clay.

LARRY

If you're as anxious to dry the grave as that
I'd better help by fanning with my hat.

[*They fan together and the* WIDOW *croons.*]

WIDOW

September keep you, Johnny,
October hold you tight,
November and December snows
Cover you soft and light.

In January the clay will sink,
The winds of February and March
Will howl around the Churchyard
And through the ruined arch;
April will swell the daffodil
And my heart, filled with Spring,
Forget the Winter and the snows
Remembering how to sing.

LARRY

If I were you I'd employ a man
To do this with an electric fan.

[*Enter the* GRAVEDIGGER.]

GRAVEDIGGER

How are you Larry? Might I enquire
Are you cooling your tea or starting a fire?

LARRY

"A fine fire when it starts!" as the fox says.
No, I'm helping this lady to dry
The clay that you piled on her husband
Who had the misfortune to die.

GRAVEDIGGER

Sure he won't notice if it's wet or dry
Any more than we will bye and bye.

WIDOW

I promised my husband that while the clay was wet
I'd never marry again, and so it's love
That keeps me here at work.

GRAVEDIGGER

                    Love is it? Love?
There's love enough in this half acre to set
A generation's poets up in stock-in-trade.
Scandals, elopements, suicides and broken hearts,

They're all one here with usury and trickery,
Villainy and bribery, corruption and depravity.
Love won't warm them now or keep them cool,
And that's a truth that should be taught at school.

WIDOW

Keep that story for the Autumn nights
Or Winter evenings, locked in bitter ice,
And tell it then to monks or sandalled friars.
The fiery kiss of love can melt the snow.

LARRY

I've often read a paper by its glow.

GRAVEDIGGER

Do you think that the poor soul on deathbed
Staring at Peter's Gate with watery eye
Would barter one half-minute of eternity
Against a bedded year with the likeliest bride
He ever held, looked after or imagined?

LARRY

Death is a mask to frighten children
Or old men doddering to the grave
But lovers at their hedge-school, loving
From kiss to kiss need not be brave,
And I . . .

WIDOW

The night is down and dew will damp
The earth that all day long I've worked to dry.

LARRY

I never knew a female yet,
Maiden, wife or widow-woman
Would let a man say out his say,
And I suppose you're only human.

You'd be amazed the brilliant thoughts,
The poems, epigrams and wit
That my wife neatly kills at birth
With, "Close the door before you sit!"

GRAVEDIGGER

Much good your wit and epigram
Will do you in your final hours,
When all the poetry you will hear
Is "R.I.P." and "Prayers, not flowers."

LARRY

The tinker dreams at night of cans,
The horsey man of hock and crupper,
And men whose livelihood is death
Can scarcely pick a bone for supper
Without a thought of graves and worms;
And, even knocking back a drink,
May see not porter in the glass
But half a pint of doomsday ink!
And men of your profound profession
Can never let the living live;
Undertaker, priest and doctor
Think every man a fugitive.

WIDOW

You'd talk the cross off twenty ass's backs.

LARRY

You'd do no good to-night I'd say,
If rain comes on your work is spoiled;
So leave your job and come with me,
The wife will have the kettle boiled.

WIDOW

Ah, perhaps I'd better; I'm very tired, my hand
Can scarcely hold the fan, my fingers ache,
My eyes are bloodshot and my hair dishevelled.

Maybe a night of sleep, a cup of tea,
A breakfast in the morning will renew
My strength.

GRAVEDIGGER
Better go home and rest and pray,
And I'll attend the grave. 'Twill only cost
Ten shillings a year. I'll plant primroses and pansies.
You'll have a garden fit for any corpse.
And come again in Spring when airs are soft,
You'll find the earth is dry, the roots well taken;
Instead of dank and dismal heavy clay
A flowered bed-spread turned down to welcome you.

And I'll be waiting with my spade in hand
To tuck you in and wish you safe good-night.
  Only the dead tucked away in the clay
  Are happy and safe till Gabriel's day.
  Only the body whose blood is cold
  Cares nothing for lust, ambition or gold;
  Only the man who's laid out straight
  Can tell disloyalty from true faith.

WIDOW

Well then poor Johnny knows my heart
And knows I've done a widow's part.
I'll come again when wind and sun
Have finished what I've well begun.

LARRY

Then let's be going. Take my arm.

WIDOW

I will and welcome. Where's the harm?

[*They go off and the curtains of the inner stage are drawn.*]

2ND TAILOR

Then up she got and away she went
And she as light as any feather.

5TH TAILOR

What would your grandmama have thought
If she had seen those two together?

2ND TAILOR

My grandmother was safe at home,
As virtuous as a sitting hen;
Not for her the cross-roads dance
Or conversations with strange men.
She was a woman of thirty-two,
Big, robust and domineering,
Who ruled her husband, ran her house—
A type that's swiftly disappearing.
She was talking with the doctor
Who called when grandpa was away . . .

1ST TAILOR

I thought you said your grandmother
Was anything but light and gay?

2ND TAILOR

Think no evil of my grandmother;
She loved the doctor as a brother!

SCENE II

The inner curtains are drawn and
MRS. LARRY *and the* DOCTOR
are discovered in LARRY'S *home;*
a backdrop suggests the scene:
a dresser, a few chairs and a
table constitute the furniture.

DOCTOR

Mrs. Larry, tell me this,
Have you ever traded kiss,
Squeeze or hug or tender sigh,
Clasp of finger, wink of eye
With a fellow such as I?

MRS. LARRY

Never, doctor, since I wed
Has any young man turned my head;
I have been entirely true
And never has the vile cuckoo
Doubled his note for such as you.

DOCTOR

Mrs. Larry, tell me then,
Do you hate the race of men?
Are you to love an infidel?
Or would you know why I excel
In what doctors know, but never tell?

MRS. LARRY

Sin grows from curiosity
Was the first thing Larry taught to me;
And I decided long ago
That I would never wish to know
Why lover's voices tremble so.

DOCTOR

Love is the only healthy sport, and love
Is education, and I've heard some say
That love's religion; for God is love, and so
In loving we are praying. Let us pray

Together, Mrs. Larry. A healthy mind
Within a healthy body is happiness,
And neither's truly healthy without love;
So love's my prescription for all nature's ills.
If I were married to you, Mrs. Larry,
'Tis long till I would leave you here alone
To be blown on by every black night wind
And frightened by every stroller. In my arms
You'd be as safe as fledgling in the nest.

MRS. LARRY

I never catch a cold, and beggarmen
Who once come skulking after night has fallen
Never return, for I've a bitter tongue;
And 'tisn't often Larry is so late . . .

DOCTOR

That sounds like him now coming through the gate . . .

[*Enter* LARRY *and the* WIDOW.]

LARRY

Evening Doctor; Hello Mary.
There's a widow-woman here
That's tired and hungry, cold and sick
Because she said she'd persevere
In drying up the cold, damp clay
Over her husband's new-made grave;
Three days so far she's on the job
Working like a nigger slave.

DOCTOR

And that's a very decent, wholesome thought,
But the churchyard for the quick is a lonesome spot.

MRS. LARRY

Bring her in to warm her bones;
That's no night for jingling knees
Upon the churchyard tombstones.

WIDOW

I'm half afraid to court the light,
My hair is tossed, my face is white.

DOCTOR

And what poor woman who has lost her husband
In the last great lottery of all regards
Her looks? Come, woman, to the fire and warm
The good life back into your empty veins
And tell us why you promised to dry the clay.

WIDOW

I never promised such a thing,
But only that I'd never wed
Until the grave had dried again
That had become his bed.

MRS. LARRY

And you intend to marry again?
Oh, shame! If Larry here should die
I'd wear my widowed black until
The world wore black for me; and I
Would drench the clay so with my tears
It would not dry for twenty years.

WIDOW

I was a faithful wife, and still
Am faithful to his memory;

But had I died and Johnny lived
I'd not expect such constancy.
The nights are cold in Winter and
Two make a warmer bed, so why
Shiver in loneliness until
The heating time of July?

MRS. LARRY

These are no thoughts to speak or even to think
Lest someone pin them to the page with ink
And spread them through the land to end all mourning
And end all patient love with ribald scorning;
Your love was not love if you can think of loving,
Your faithfulness was easy of removing.

WIDOW

I am too tired to argue, let me be.

LARRY

I promised the poor girl a cup of tea.

MRS. LARRY

I will be silent since she is your guest
And only think more bitterly the rest.
Come then and warm your body, heat your
    blood.

LARRY

Let's go and get the girl a bit of food.

[*They go, and after a moment the* DOCTOR *goes to the window and makes a signal.* SEAMUS *enters.*]

SEAMUS

Here is the phial you ordered with the brew
Of deadly drugs distilled and double-distilled
Which only the Italian Borgias knew
And used when supper guests were to be killed.
Long in a withered book the secret hid
Like the flushed vampire that for centuries lies.
One drop upon the eyelid blinds, one drop
Mixed with the food and all the company dies.

DOCTOR

I fear the key to pleasure comes too late
For the giant Honour guards that gate.
However, I'll not weep to see him die
And perhaps will breach the fortress bye and bye,
To which for two years I have brought artillery,
Reinforcements, great field weapons, infantry
To batter down those walls.

                          Seamus, I dream
Of the capitulation, terms made, war ended
And the commander-in-chief in the chief palace
Entertained by the sweetest foe that ever fought—
And in this phial is the father of that thought.

SEAMUS

I'm a man that's an adept at playing that game,
And however it's played the result is the same—
I've courted them old and I've courted them young,
I've courted a slut with a vinegar tongue,
I've courted wee lassies as high as your knee
And I've courted an old one a hundred and three.
I've brought them small presents and I've
      brought them great,
I've played them and hooked them with varying
      bait,

I've landed fat widows, young wives and old maids
For mine is the best of all slouthering trades,
I've fooled them and kissed them and kept them at play
Till the cock blew Reveille the following day—
But the finest of fish are the ones that escape
And the sweetest of fruit is the ungathered grape.

DOCTOR

Here in the bottle we'll drop the good sup
And Larry will soon fill himself the last cup;
And once he is bundled from mind and from sight
Mrs. Larry will soon find it cold in the night.

SEAMUS

Hurry up, for I hear them returning again;
So in with the poison.

DOCTOR

So be it, and Amen.

[LARRY, MRS. LARRY *and the* WIDOW *return.*]

WIDOW

Now I feel a better woman,
Now once more I'm nearly human;
Where in the world can any find
A better poultice for the mind?

LARRY

There was never a thing like a cup of tea
To put the heart of life in me;

A heat by the fire and a sup of punch
Would put a head on the greatest dunce;
A sup of punch and good company
Are better again than a cup of tea.

MRS. LARRY

I never believed in stimulants
Backache powders or liniments;
Clear spring water and wheaten bread
And eight good hours in a feather bed . . .

DOCTOR

Eight good hours in a feather bed,
A sneeze in the morning to clear the head—
Whoever tries this experiment
Need use no powder, paint or scent.

LARRY

But a sup of malt when a man's well fed
Gives extra curves to a feather bed;
Here's the bottle and here's the cup,
Will you join me Doctor in a sup?

DOCTOR

Old Mother Nature for my sins
Has given a patient a pair of twins,
And by my reckoning this is the night
When they are due to come to light.

LARRY

Tell me, Seamus, will you drink?
There's twice the pleasure when glasses clink;
Then taste and touch and sight and smell
Are joined by hearing that laughing bell.

SEAMUS

I took the pledge when I was young
And never has my pointed tongue
Lapped porter, whiskey, wine.
So pardon me if I decline.

LARRY

Good fortune then; here's luck; here's health.
In fact, here's everything but wealth.

DOCTOR

Here in the glass the future glows.

LARRY

Tip her up and down she goes.

[*He drinks.*]

WIDOW

He's turning pale; he's sweating at the pores.
He drops the glass, throws back his head and snores.
And now the eyes are turning in his head.

[*The* DOCTOR *feels his pulse very cursorily.*]

DOCTOR

Unless I'm much mistaken he is dead.

MRS. LARRY

Dead did you say? Dead did you mean?
Hold a mirror to his lips.
Whiskey may kill by inches
But it never kills by sips.

[SEAMUS *holds a mirror to* LARRY'S *mouth.*]

SEAMUS

This mirror, which delights in apeing
Man and his hundred actions, sees
Nothing to counterfeit in him—
Prepare his obsequies.

DOCTOR

I'm very much afraid he's gone
Where Winter, Summer, Spring
Have all one climate, and the Autumn
Brings no cool weather in.

MRS. LARRY

Dead did you say? Now rain come pouring down
From every sullen cloud, now wave on shore
Moan with my grief, now garden strip of leaf
And flower, and mourn in nakedness. To think
A little golden drop could rip like lightning

Through the fabric of his life and leave me only
An empty, punctured bag drooped on the floor.
Mourn for my man who grew beside me, sturdy
In every weather, brave to the wind, alert
To all dark sounds of night, prepared for any
Enemy but this, this treason in
His pleasure cup, his little laughing drop.

DOCTOR

This is the hand that waits on every landing
To trip the foot. Larry's a lucky man
To die in company, in gusty mirth.
Not for him the wrinkled sheet, the sour
Unrested head, the table rich with bottles.
Death took him suddenly as one might take
A glass of sherry at a friendly wake.

WIDOW

He's with my Johnny, and it's strange
That two young men who never met
Are thrown together now forever,
Caught in the same net.

MRS. LARRY

Laughter was frothy in this room awhile,
Concealing, like the cuckoo-spit, green death
That now slips in and bleaches all the colours.
Empty on their racks the suits are hanging,
Mere foolish cloth whose meaning was their wearer;
And this poor empty body that was shining
Craves only a small freehold of the earth.
Send for the neighbours, hang crape upon the door;
But let me creep to a corner of the mind
Until the coffin thumps upon the stair.

33

DOCTOR

Send for the Undertaker now,
The Priest and echoing Clerk;
Roll in the barrels, fill the house
With all traditional carouse
To keep away the dark.

SEAMUS

Call in the neighbours to the fire,
Give every man a pipe and glass
And let him smoke and drink and smile
Rejoicing that he lives awhile,
Fanned by the wings that pass.

DOCTOR

The man that's dead would grudge no man
Another while to walk the earth;
He'd be the first to fill a can—
So let us drink his health again
At his hospitable hearth.

SEAMUS [to the audience.]

Good friends, I bring you sorry news;
Poor Larry's dead. Come mourn with us,
Shake Mrs. Larry's hand and say,
How swift, how sad, how soon it was.
Walk to the room and see him stretched
Cold in the bed where he was hot,
Then kneel and pray in gratitude
That he is dead and you are not.

DOCTOR

Come to the wake-house, change your tie,
Take from the shelf the dismal face,
Prepare to droop the mournful eye
And slow the living, youthful pace.

And when your duty words are said
Tobacco waits, and wine and cakes,
Whiskey and stout and living men
To light your wit up—Come to the wake.

SEAMUS
Come to the wake and say, 'Alas!
My dearest friend, the bravest best . . .
But he is in a better place,
Secure with Him that knows the rest.'
Say, 'He is free from bills and bores,
A dazzling soul in purest white
Preparing for eternity
Of nightless day and dayless night.'

DOCTOR
But as you speak relish the heat
That circulates about your bones—
Eternity for you may be
Unending gnashing, endless groans.
Then, as you pass the bottle, think
That still your senses pleasure take
In all the foolish weaknesses
That are forbidden—Come to the wake.

[*Enter* GRAVEDIGGER.]

GRAVEDIGGER
Come to the wake. Come to the wake.
The greatest pleasure is a fake.
You cannot have and eat your cake.
Death watches in at every chink,
He's in the pleasure-cup you drink
And every epigram you make
Says, Come to the wake. Come to the wake.

[*The inner curtains are drawn.*]

2ND TAILOR

And so he died. The house was readied
To bring the neighbours in;
The hams were bought, the barrels brought
The whiskey and the gin,
Clay pipes with greedy, droughty mouths
And high-grade snuff *go leor*
The neighbour women laid him out,
The neighbour men with thoughts of stout
Were lounging at the door.

1ST TAILOR

That was a wake to please the mind,
But what dead man to-day
Can say he's waked in proper style?
The neighbours kneel and pray,
But dance or song we're told is wrong,
The dumb piano stands
Grim as a coffin all night long,
The flesh is weak, but memory's strong
And longest in this land.

5TH TAILOR

All summer long I've stitched and cut
And sewn the buttons on,
My legs are cramped, but thought is free
And youth must have its fun;
I'd jump a five-barred gate, and I
Could leap a mile in thought,
So why not jump back fifty years
To snuff and hams and pipes and beers
That our forefathers bought?

2ND TAILOR

Time is a name to frighten children
Or old men near the grave,
But youth can catch his withered beard
And drag him from his cave.

1ST TAILOR

And even Time must bow to those
Who snip and cut and weave.
The Fates who tailor life as we
Shape trouser-leg or sleeve.

2ND TAILOR

These three old women rule us all,
Clotho and Atropos
And Lachesis; call on their power
To ferry us across.

5TH TAILOR [*intones*]

Aunt Clotho come, Aunt Atropos
And kind Aunt Lachesis;
Lend us a skiey horse with wings
To leap Time's precipice.

6TH TAILOR

I'll not indulge in any magic,
And I'll tell Father Pat
The kind of goings on that's going . . .

[*There is a flash of lightning and a peal of thunder.*]

Oh murder! What was that?

4TH TAILOR

I'll not believe that Time is fluid,
Time was, Time is, will be;
A day once slipped into the past
Has joined eternity.

[*Lightning, thunder, complete darkness.*]

3RD TAILOR

Either a storm is blowing up
Or we are blowing down.
Wings are about us and the past
Vivid as when men drown.

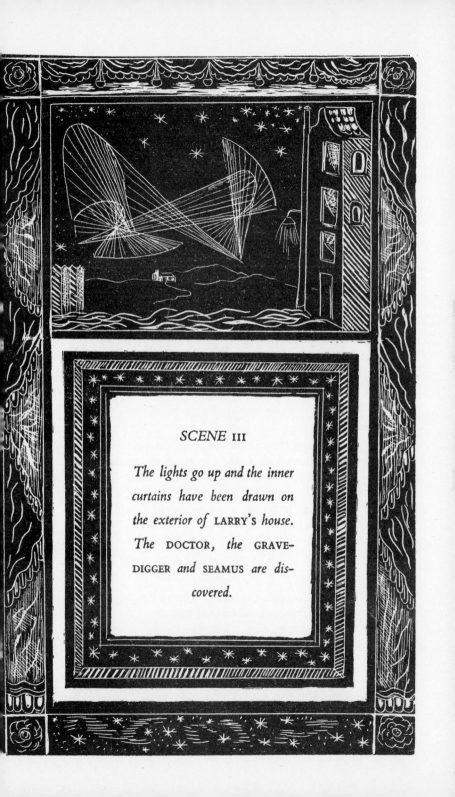

SCENE III

*The lights go up and the inner
curtains have been drawn on
the exterior of* LARRY'S *house.
The* DOCTOR, *the* GRAVE-
DIGGER *and* SEAMUS *are discovered.*

5TH TAILOR

Aunt Atropos has cut the thread
That binds us in to-day.
Come to the wake, boys, join the gang.
To-day is yesterday.

SEAMUS

Will you come along and join us
And walk into the parlour,
There's whiskey and tobacco there
And port wine for the ladies;
You're six strange men I never saw
This side of Ireland's island
But you're welcome to the wake-house one
    and all.

DOCTOR

If I hadn't got my glasses on
I'd say that they were babies
Although they're standing upright
And have clothes that's fit for gentlemen;
But there's something of the innocence
Of birth about their faces,
But they're welcome to the wake-house one
    and all.

GRAVEDIGGER

I wouldn't say they're strangers
And I wouldn't say they're neighbours,
But they've a look of you and me
A familiar cast of countenance—
They're Yanks, maybe, some neighbours' sons
Were born across the water,
But they're welcome to the wake-house one
    and all.

1ST TAILOR

It's hard to understand it,
But we're the golden future
That lights the gloomy day for you,
A Christmassy shop window,
We're the sons that you have fathered
Between two walls of darkness
But we're coming to the wake-house just the
    same.

DOCTOR

May I introduce the pharmacist,
And this our grave gravedigger
I'm the doctor, and the three of us
Assist men in and out of life.

[SEAMUS *and the* GRAVEDIGGER *shake hands
and then wander away.*]

I'll not believe your story
And as a psycho-analyst
I'd say you weren't too steady in the brain.

2ND TAILOR

Larry is my grandfather
And I know all the twist of it,
The silver words you whisper
In my grandma's golden ear,
The little drop that Seamus there
Slipped in the *deoch a' doruis*—
And what's to follow after is as plain.

DOCTOR

I'll poison you, I'll shoot you,
I'll carve you into gobbets;

41

Your flesh will melt like water
Your livers turn to stone.
Seamus will kick your heads like balls
From here to Ballyferriter—
As I said before you must be all insane.

5TH TAILOR

We're the future, and untouchable,
And some of us not born at all;
We're here to see the finish
Of this tragedy or comedy.
Pretend we never happened,
Scrape our faces from your memory—
But we're coming to the wake-house just the
    same.

[*They go off and* SEAMUS *and the* GRAVEDIGGER *rejoin the* DOCTOR.]

DOCTOR

I thought that I was talking
To six madmen for an instant,
But they were humorous fellows
Who were anxious for a joke.
I'm sure poor Mrs. Larry
Will be anxious for my company—
I'd better hurry back and stake my claim.

GRAVEDIGGER

Thoughts of death should be your comrades
As you walk the house of death,
The cloistered eye and rigid mouth
Remind you that your breath

Might falter in an instant—
This evening Larry laughed,
Called Death a children's bogeyman
But which of us was daft?

DOCTOR

Before that bogey catches me
I'll thank him for his courtesy
In clearing roads before me
That were guarded well and jealously.
Death is a friend to servants who
Walk in his footsteps cautiously,
I'll hail him as the god of love
Whose bolt was shot unerringly.

SEAMUS

Here's herself arrayed in black
Stepping from the back-door,
Walking in the shadowed eaves;
The noisy woe of those she leaves
Follows her through every crack
And meets her at the front door.

DOCTOR

Fatherly and humanly
I'll speak to her most courteously,
Half a priest and half a man;
No half suspicion of my plan
Will loiter even fleetingly
Until she's grown all womanly.

[SEAMUS *and the* GRAVEDIGGER *go as* MRS. LARRY
approaches, walking at the back of the stage.]

Mrs. Larry, do you wander
In the night-time unattended,
Loveless in your grieving time,
In the dark time unbefriended?
A fate like yours might make us wonder
Whether God beholds the sparrow
And leaves poor man to stumble dark
Into a pit of sorrow.
Do not resent the arm that presses
Your widowed waist, its innocence
Is as the veil that shields your beauty
From every light offence;
And if my lips should touch your ear
In whispering a grieving word
Think it no more than if the sky
Caress a widowed bird;
And if my tears should stain your cheek
Think that the self-same grief
Reddens our eyelids. Heart to heart
Let sorrow be our chief.
Ah, do not take the hand I kiss
In sorrowing friendship, rather leave
Those five poor fingers in my five
And let the decade weave
A rosary; and do not wander
So by night-time unattended.
While I am at your side you'll find
All your grieving thoughts befriended.

Friendship is sometimes more than love,
In friendship there's no jealousy,
No crazed possession of the loved,
No passionate redundancy.
In friendship I could kiss your lips,
Could hold you in my arms embraced,

My hands might wander, but my blood
Be like spring water, cool and chaste.
You are no wanton like that widow
Whose death-room thoughts were gay,
Who squandered hours of weeping time
In comforting the clay.
No man can ever jostle Larry
Out of your mind I know,
No thought of marriage-bed can mar
The friendship that I owe
To Larry's memory, no other ring
Can ever dominate your finger;
So, if I kiss your salted lips,
Permit my lips to linger.

MRS. LARRY

I have spoken of faithfulness to memory,
Of eternal widowhood and mourning garments,
But now, with Larry stretched and suddenly dead,
The hours filled up with mourners, winter in
The bedroom and the misery of remembrance
Standing in every object in the room
I begin to wonder if my heart can be
So fixed, so constant.
                          My ship is captainless,
No star, no astrolabe, no chart—*Marie
Celeste* I stagger blindfold on my course
Lost between continents of memory.
There's no one now to grasp my half-seized thought,
To tease my sleepy silence, no one now . . .

DOCTOR

But, Mrs. Larry, you have me,
All thoughtfulness and sympathy.

45

MRS. LARRY

It isn't the thoughtfulness and sympathy
That break my heart for Larry, but the million
Mornings and evenings, the toothbrush by the
    mirror,
The nightshirt on the floor, the tiny actions.

DOCTOR

Wouldn't it be pleasant,
Be pleasant and delightful
If all you've lost you could regain,
Fill every jug and glass full
And find that life was right again
And pleasant and delightful.
The blood that's pumping from my heart
Is salty, rich and red,
My nose not pinched in pointed death
And if I cannot catch my breath
It's all because my moidered head
Is overflowing, packed and full
With images of board and bed
Most pleasant and delightful.
The leaden casket round your heart
Is crushing it to death now,
Smash it and leap to life again—
That's breaking up no marriage-vow;
The lips that once were dedicate
To Larry, now are free to kiss,
Kiss me, and, in parenthesis,
Change wine of love for watered hate,
Fill every jug and glass full
It's pleasant and delightful.

MRS. LARRY

Doctor, your words go stamping through my heart
Smashing china and delicate bric-à-brac;

All's in a storm, the curtains floating free
And I'm afraid what may become of me.
All that was bright and tidy, known and safe
Is suddenly blown down and I without a home.

DOCTOR

Trust your medical adviser to know best,
Come into my waiting, loving arms and rest.

[*They embrace, the curtains are drawn on the inner
stage and the tailors appear on the outer.*]

2ND TAILOR

The dirty dog. I knew his scheme.

1ST TAILOR

The dirty murderer you mean.

4TH TAILOR

The dirty bowsey is what I'd say.

5TH TAILOR

The dirty scut has got away
With murder and seduction too.
Well, boys, what are we going to do?

2ND TAILOR

We're the future, and I'm doubtful
That we can meddle in the past,
This play is fifty years of age
And we're not even in the cast.

But maybe what is happening now
Did happen fifty years ago
And maybe if we take a part
We can assure our future too.
There's a little poisoned bottle
On the shelf inside the room,
There's a glass or two of liquor going round
And a broken-hearted woman wanders under-
    neath the moon,
And the god of love forever gazes down.
Now if one of us could nobble
That little poisoned drop
And pour it in the doctor's glass of malt
The doctor and his scheming and his wicked
    heart would stop—
So come on boys—which of you is worth his
    salt?

5TH TAILOR

I wouldn't be a murderer and
Risk my precious soul,
But seeing as the man is dead
I'll pass the poisoned bowl.
If the man is dead a second death
Can do him little injury . . .

2ND TAILOR

And if he's not we'll constitute
His hangman, judge and jury.

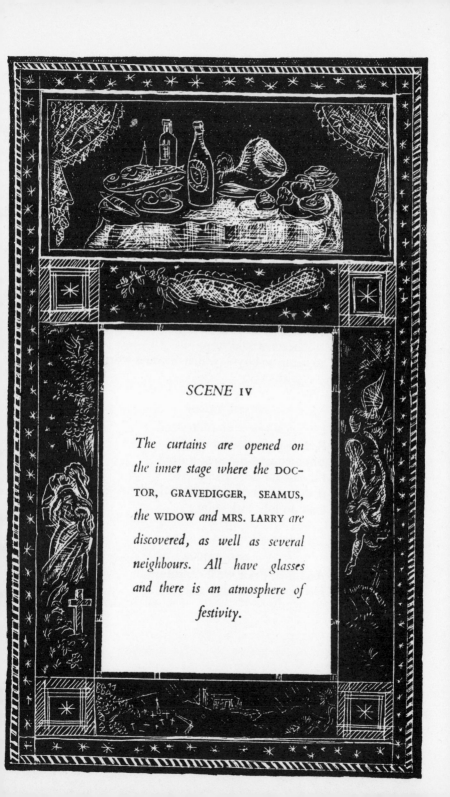

SCENE IV

The curtains are opened on the inner stage where the DOC-
TOR, GRAVEDIGGER, SEAMUS,
the WIDOW *and* MRS. LARRY *are
discovered, as well as several
neighbours. All have glasses
and there is an atmosphere of
festivity.*

DOCTOR

Cease to mourn now, cease to mourn,
The wake is over and grief is gone,
Larry is dead and weeping eyes
Will bed him no softer in paradise,
And if he's gone to another place
He'll not be cooled down by a mournful face.
I've good news, best news, news of joy,
This is the gold without alloy,
This is the wine of the vintage year,
This is the story with never a tear.
Put back that mask upon the wall,
Rejoice with me, laugh one, laugh all,
Larry is dead, but his widow is not,
Her eyes are sparkling, her blood is hot.
Put away, put away that doleful mask,
Sing with me, sing with me, all I ask
Is life for death, resurrection,
Let this be a gold collection.
Larry alive meant little to you,
Little to me, but dead it's true
He becomes a symbol and we weep
For the pretty life we cannot keep.
I've good news, strange news, the best ever known,
Joy is returned and sorrow is gone,
This wake will turn to a wedding tune
For Mrs. Larry will marry me soon.

GRAVEDIGGER

O shame! O most disgraceful conduct! This
Dethrones death and enthrones concupisence.
In this room are gathered neighbours who,
Respecting old tradition and their friend,
Speak only good of Larry who is gone;
Whatever bitter scorpion malice rears
Is for a season drugged, and Larry wrapped
In silk and satin glory for his passing.

HAPPY AS LARRY

You talk of marriage while the blood is still
Fluid within his veins, not yet so sluggish
That a miracle-word might not restore him living.
And do you say that Mrs. Larry now,
Forgetting duty and the grief she owes
Can think of lust? I'll not be party to
This impious flouting of experience.

DOCTOR

Because the husband's death is that a reason
Why, Indian-like, the wife should perish too?

WIDOW

Because I worked to dry the cold grave-clay
This woman called me wanton, but I obeyed
My husband's dying words. Her husband's grave
Is not yet dug and yet she calls the banns.

I begin to feel that perhaps the event has shown
That I was the loyal wife who made no promise
But loved in steadfastness and was prepared
To love again. My Johnny knew it all
And only asked a widow's mite of sorrow.

SEAMUS

Whatever's happy, whatever's gay
Is virtuous and good;
Whatever's ill and sodden-eyed
Is evil to the blood.
What man has ever courted sorrow
When joy was courting him?
What man has hankered after Winter
With Spring in leaf and limb?
        'Twill be pleasant and delightful
When the fire is heaped again,
When the bottle in the evening
Makes a tent against the rain;
As pleasant as the Summer
When the sun appears to stand
Day long above the hayfield
Till the fairest cheek is tanned
And the hair is bleached like linen,
The earth ripened and caressed
Till the ageing hand of Autumn
Plucks the roses from her breast.
Then pleasant, Oh, most pleasant
The vigil of the Spring
When the heart gropes upward
Toward's the year's replenishing,
Till joy bursts through in crocus
And the earth becomes a bower
Of daffodil and hawthorn,
Almond and cherry-flower.

WIDOW

But sorrow also has its season,
My Johnny's dead and I
Will wait to take another
Till his cold grave-clay is dry.

DOCTOR

And that's a chorus that I'm tired of,
All you need is a man
And then the grave and the teary eye
Can dry as best they can.

MRS. LARRY

I was the loyallest wife that ever
Wore a wedding-ring,
And I was ready to mourn until
My coffin was hammering;
But the doctor assures me that doctors know
The poison that thins the blood,
And if I marry it's only because
He's convinced it will do me good.
I'll pray every night for Larry's safe keeping
In heaven or purgatory,
And if he's gone where my prayers can't help,
Why then they may help me.
Larry is dead, your Johnny is dead
And there's many another gone,
And if we had waited a year or two
We could be blamed by none.
But in widowhood an hour of weeping
May equal a year as a wife,
And the doctor says a widow unmarried
Insults her married life,
Saying in black that her husband failed
Both at board and bed—
And loving my Larry as I did
I'll not insult the dead.
   [*Enter the* TAILORS.]

6TH TAILOR

Oh, Mrs. Larry
You should be ashamed of yourself!
What will all the neighbours say?
You should be on the shelf.
You find yourself a husband
With the old one scarcely gone,
And oh! Mrs. Larry,
You surely know it's wrong.

1ST TAILOR

Oh, Mrs. Larry,
You should be ashamed of your life,
As tree and bark are allied
So are a man and wife;
I've never seen a widow
So soon a husband take,
And oh! Mrs. Larry,
What will become of the wake?

5TH TAILOR

Oh, Mrs. Larry,
What will the clergy say?
They'll think it isn't decent
If you want to wed to-day;
The priest who comes to bury
Will scarcely stay to wed,
And Oh! Mrs. Larry
It isn't time for bed.

4TH TAILOR

Oh, Mrs. Larry,
What will the doctor think?
In a month or two he'll wonder
Which was the weakest link;

54

And maybe he'll consider
That such a rusted chain
If once it could be parted
Might easily snap again.

3RD TAILOR

And oh! Mrs. Larry,
Warning take from me,
The apple that is sweetest
Is highest on the tree;
The open city captured
Is thought no victory,
Takes no place in history
With *Veni, Vidi, Vici!*

2ND TAILOR

Oh, Mrs. Larry,
Consider posterity,
Though the Doctor speaks to your heart now
The future speaks through me;
The gun you hold is loaded,
The drink is poisoned drink,
The house is mined, the warrants signed,
So pause a while and think.

DOCTOR

Think no longer, think no more,
Thought is the enemy of joy,
The heart knows best what road to take,
Change funeral meats for wedding cake
And make me Larry's viceroy.

MRS. LARRY

I'm frightened of these gentlemen
Who spoke so very strangely.

DOCTOR

I know how to deal with them,
A drink will very quickly stem
Their flood of whimsicality.
            [*To the* TAILORS].
So fill the tankards, fill the pots,
Drink to Mrs. Larry's eyes,
Drink to me and drink to you,
Drink to what we're going to do;
Drink to your shocked surprise.
Here men, fill your glasses up.

5TH TAILOR

Will you join us, doctor, in a sup?
[*The* TAILORS *go into a huddle in the front of the stage.*]

3RD TAILOR

Fill the doctor the best in the house.

2ND TAILOR

Fill the doctor the very best drink.

4TH TAILOR

Fill him a glass that'll curl his toes,
Fill it with doomsday ink.

1ST TAILOR

Fill him a ball of brimstone malt
Triple-distilled from the tears of the damned
That'll melt his bones and curdle his blood
And crackle his skin till Hell's door is slammed.

6TH TAILOR

Arsenic, strychnine, sulphuric acid,
Poison distilled from the rankest root,
Hyoscine and Chemist's bane
That fatten the gallows with annual fruit;

56

Pour it out for him, sour flat stout for him,
Bluestone poteen, claret cup,
Christmas whiskey laced with Red Biddy,
Bath-brewed beer and Johnny Jump-Up.

2ND TAILOR

And here is worse for him, here's my curse for him,
May his tongue be as dry as St. Patrick's Day
And the devils scratch it for striking matches
While pints of good porter around him spray.

5TH TAILOR

It's time he started on his way,
Blow the whistle, wave the flag,
There is no stop this side of Hell.
    [*To the* DOCTOR]
Carry your bag, mister, carry your bag.

DOCTOR

I'm not going anywhere,
I invite you to a drink
And all you do is gossip there.

5TH TAILOR

I know, our manners stink.

DOCTOR

Pull the corks now, fill the glass,
To all the sensual world proclaim,
A marriage with thy neighbour's wife
Is worth an age without a dame.

[*The* FIFTH TAILOR *takes the poisoned bottle, and as he pours it and then as it is passed by one* TAILOR *to the other the following verses are spoken.*]

2ND TAILOR

Come and watch the birdie
Take his little sip
Between the hand and bottle,
Between the glass and lip,
Between the lip and throttle
There can be many a slip.

4TH TAILOR

Come and watch the birdie
Take his glass of malt,
Between the dish and finger,
Between the meat and salt
It's possible to linger
To make a fatal fault.

3RD TAILOR

Pour it for the birdie
Never spill a sip,
Careful with the bottle,
The glass goes to the lip,
He pours it down his throttle--
Here's to auld acquaintanceship.

[*As the next verses are spoken the* TAILORS *and* NEIGH-
BOURS *dance in a ring around the* DOCTOR *who is standing
dazed in the centre of the stage.*]

5TH TAILOR

Dance, dance the doctor's dance,
Old tradition's desecrated,
Forget the dance of death and prance
Like Harlem hoodlums liberated.

1ST TAILOR

Dance, dance the doctor's dance,
Joy, he says, is reinstated,
See the bright new age advance,
Civilized, sophisticated.

4TH TAILOR

Dance, dance the doctor's dance,
Soon he will be liquidated,
Send for the nurse and ambulance
That wait on the intoxicated.

3RD TAILOR

Dance, dance the doctor's dance,
I fear it's almost terminated,
Notice the wildness of his glance
Which indicates he's addle-pated.

6TH TAILOR

Dance no more, he has the stance
Of one whose heart's incinerated;
He's trying to make utterance
Although he's more than spiflicated.

[*The dancing stops suddenly and the* DOCTOR *speaks in a very hoarse voice.*]

DOCTOR

Here's your very good health,
Here's very good cheer.
Damn it, what's in the bottle?
My head isn't clear.
My brain-pan is melting,
My heart's turned to stone.
Damn it *what's* in the bottle?
Oh damn it, I'm done.

VOICES

Oh, what's happened?
He's going to die.
He's dead already.
That's all my eye.
Stand back, give him air.
Smelling-salts, water,
Hot-bottles. A chair.
It must be his heart.
A stroke maybe.
Did he mix his drinks?
Bring a cup of tea.

SEAMUS

For what ails him this minute there's only one cure,
It's quick and it's certain and never has failed;
Quick blood from the living can save him from death—
Who'll give him a pint before he has paled?

GRAVEDIGGER

I'll not be over-anxious to venture my life
In meddling with death. What death grapples on
Is better abandoned. If one victim escaped
The next life Death demanded might well be my own.

SEAMUS

The Doctor's my friend and I'm willing to drain
A pint of hot blood from the first volunteer
And pump it in steaming to rally his heart.
The knife's sharp and ready. What bids do I hear?

MRS. LARRY

I'd be first with my offer, but I'm not too sure
That my blood-group is right. What's wrong with
        your own?
Or there's men here with gallons of blood they could
        spare
Whom stout and high living have much overblown.

SEAMUS

I'd be first with my offer myself if I could,
But I handle the knife and it wouldn't be right.
Hurry up, if the blood gets congealed in his veins
You can order his coffin. We can't wait all night.

WIDOW

There wasn't much talk of transfusion of blood
When Larry was dying, his symptoms the same;
I'll not venture my life on the point of your knife,
You could have saved Larry if that was your aim.

SEAMUS

Bedamn, I forgot that the blood of a man
Who isn't long dead is as good as my own;
I'll puncture his heart and draw off a quart—
Poor Larry was healthy and his wild oats well sown.

2ND TAILOR

You'll do no such a thing you murdering villain,
'Twas yourself and the doctor that murdered the man;
You'll not get your hands on his body I'll warrant you
I'll have him carved up by no charlatan.

GRAVEDIGGER

Oh, loathsome, unnatural, bestial crime.
And why did they murder the innocent lad?

5TH TAILOR

Not for money or power, but to get for the Doctor
His wife, the one treasure the poor fellow had.

MRS. LARRY

I'll not believe there's murder done,
My Larry died as men must die,
So, Seamus, if you need the blood
Take it from Larry speedily.

5TH TAILOR

The only thing that killed the doctor
Was his and Seamus's villainy;
I fed him from the poisoned bottle
He's dead of his own whiskey.

GRAVEDIGGER

There's double murder, double death.
Oh horror! Oh, most vicious times!
The Decalogue is smashed and now
Crime fathers nameless crimes.

WIDOW

Send for the guards and coroner
To investigate their death;
Send for the crime reporter
Let him rewrite *Macbeth*.

3RD TAILOR

We're the future and untouchable,
Judge, jury, hangman, court of appeal;
The doctor's dead at our decree
    [*To the* GRAVEDIGGER.]
Stop gaping like an imbecile.

GRAVEDIGGER

Often at night I see the ghosts
Of those who lived before us climb
Out of the grave to take the air
Until the cock cries parting-time;
And, watching those dusty figures drift
Under the moonlight, have no fear,
For they are now as we will be
When we have passed our final year.
But you six men with innocent eyes
And faces showing no map of care
To guide the traveller frighten me,
For you are now as we once were.

2ND TAILOR

We are the first explorers, the pioneers that came
Out of the virgin country, our flag's a question-mark
Quandry is our name, our sun and moon are dark,
Our faces featureless, our country unnamed.
All that you're doing now is done this fifty years,
The murderer and victim picked clean in the same earth
The laughter and the tears, the misery and mirth
Are nothing but a story to titillate our ears.
Every action is predestined, you do what you must,
Like God, we stand in loneliness anatomising dust.

MRS. LARRY

Enough of this squawk,
Give over the talk,
Is the Doctor to die
While you squabble and squall?

63

I don't care if you're heroes
From Rio de Janeiro,
Just shut your big mouths
And put an end to the brawl.

GRAVEDIGGER

There's murder done, your husband's dead,
And would you save his murderer,
This villainous pill-poisoner,
This moribund adulterer?

MRS. LARRY

I've enough of your chat
And I know what I'm at,
If you won't use the knife
I've a pin in my hat.
So give over your brawling,
Your sneers and cat-calling,
And I'll puncture his heart
If I'll only be let.

6TH TAILOR

Let her away to do her worst,
A wilful woman is born accursed;
Her story's written and all you say
Won't move her one inch out of her way.
She was the loyallest woman, she said,
That ever warmed a marriage-bed,
But look at her now that her husband's dead,
A shameless, bawdy widow instead.

MRS. LARRY

And am I bawdy in wanting to save
One out of two from an early grave?
Will you all stand by and let the man die
Then drop your tears from a hypocrite eye?

WIDOW

I was strolling through my life
With my husband by my side
When death came in between us
And suddenly Johnny died.
Death's a bold rogue, a bad rogue,
A rogue of high degree,
But if I caught one glimpse of him
He'd be no match for me.

5TH TAILOR

You walked into this house to-night
With Larry by your side,
He took one sip of whiskey
And he soon went glassy-eyed.

WIDOW

Death's a bold rogue, a bad rogue,
A rogue of high degree,
But if I'd time to see his face
He'd be no match for me.

2ND TAILOR

The Doctor thought he'd mastered Death
And had him on his side,
But Death put out his hand for him
And took him in his stride.

WIDOW

Death's a bold rogue, a bad rogue,
A rogue of high degree,
But if I stared him eye to eye
He'd be no match for me.

4TH TAILOR

He's come and gone like lightning
Or the turning of the tide,
A flicker of the eyelid
And he has you caught and tied.

WIDOW

He's a bold rogue, a bad rogue,
A rogue of high degree,
But while I'm young and in my health
He'll be no match for me.

GRAVEDIGGER

Death is in your blood this instant,
He walks beneath your skin,
You drank him with your earliest milk—
You cannot fight and win.

MRS. LARRY

He'll be no match for me,
I'll fight him and I'll win,
So, Seamus, give the knife to me
And show where I begin.

SEAMUS

You must make an incision
With care and precision,
A knick that in time
May save ninety-nine.
I've a chart that will show
The way you must go
And how you must drain
The hot blood from his brain.

3RD TAILOR

I'll not pretend that I agree
To teaching her anatomy . . . .

SEAMUS

Then you make a new incision
With courage and decision,
Pour the blood in with precision.
And in less than five minutes you'll see him alive.

MRS. LARRY

Then hand me the scalpel till I make him revive.
[*She takes the knife from* SEAMUS *and goes into the
next room.*]

2ND TAILOR

There she goes, the door is shut,
Close your eyes and see her work,
She tests the blade, the dangerous slut,
A woman fit for Hare or Burke,
Opens Larry's waistcoat, coat,
Opens the shirt and then the vest
Feels the flesh still warm and soft
On her husband's hairy chest,
Reads the chart and marks the spot,
Puts the knife against the skin,
Closes her eyes and presses hard
Feeling the keen blade sinking in.
There's blood around her fingers now,
Blood in a spout about her hand,
She opens her eyes to grab a cup,
Looks at her murdered husband and . . .
    [*There is a scream from offstage.*]

VOICES

What frightened her? What did she see?
She must have fainted, carry her out.
The door is locked, I can't get in,
What did she see? Why did she shout?
[*There is a pause, then steps can be heard coming to the
door and eventually it opens and* LARRY *appears, very
bloodstained. Shouts and screams from those on stage.*]

GRAVEDIGGER

O God in Heaven, the ghosts are out
And it not nearly twelve of the night;
In all my years of churchyard matins
I've never seen a bloodier sight.

SEAMUS

I'm sorry Larry. I didn't mean it.
Give us a chance and I'll repent,
Crawl on my knees through Lough Derg's stones,
Give up cigarettes for the whole of Lent.

GRAVEDIGGER

Are you a ghost or are you a man?
Are you alive or dead?
If you're the Larry that we know
Who's stretched within on the bed?

LARRY

I'm as dead as mutton this very minute,
Dead as a doornail, dead as Queen Anne—
Give us a drink for Moses' sake,
I'm hardly able to stand.
I can hear my heart, like a cheap alarum,
My guts are twisted, my muscles are bound,
There's fried onions sizzling in my ears,
There isn't an organ sound.
I'm as stiff as Nelson above on his pillar,
As weak as the watery drops of bad plain,
My eyes are burnt out like cigarette butts,
Will yis draw us a drink or I'll faint.
Was it brandy I drank on top of whiskey,
Or poteen brewed from Connachtmen's socks,
Or Lunatic Soup or American hooch,
Or was I learning to box?
Oh my blood is spilt and my brain is melting,
And you want to know am I living or dead.
And where's my missus in all this ruction,
Will yis give us a drink I said!

SEAMUS

You're dead, so lie down and leave us in peace,
I'd rather be tried and be hanged in Mountjoy
Than listen to ghosts come foraging liquor,
So back to your Hellfire my fine devil's boy.

LARRY

Stop your prattling, stop your talk,
Here's my hands for you to feel.
That one's steel and that one's iron,
And here's the one to make you squeal.
    [*He hits* SEAMUS.]

2ND TAILOR

Lorry him up he's no relation!
Give him a blow or two for me.
H.O.H.A., Hit one, hit all,
Here's when the wake becomes a spree.

GRAVEDIGGER

The Doctor is dead or very near it,
He must be waked—*de mortuis nil!*
I hear no sound from Mrs. Larry
And it's not like her to stay so still.

LARRY

What's going on here? What's all the talk?
Who's been poisoned? Where's my wife?
I must have drunk for half a dozen,
I've the worst hangover of all my life.

WIDOW

The Doctor and Seamus poisoned you;
The Doctor drank from the poisoned can,
Your wife went off to carve you up
Thinking your blood would cure your man.

LARRY

My head's not right, my ears are moidered,
Who in the world would want me dead;
Sure I haven't a tosser to my name
Only what I make at the cobbling trade.

6TH TAILOR

'Twas the Doctor that wanted to marry your missus,
And the same one was only too willing, I'd say,
She hadn't you cold till she was out courting
And would have been married before it was day.

LARRY

Come coroners and judges,
Come slaveys, drabs and drudges,
Come counsellors, attorneys and the press,
Come jurymen and peelers,
Come pocket-picking stealers,
Come murderers and perjurers and the rest;
Come and tell us that this story
Is neither strange nor gory,
That wives carve up their husbands every day,
That poison's drunk like tea
And that what has happened me
Wouldn't even make the action of a play.

5TH TAILOR

Come tabloid-paper readers,
Come languid fashion-leaders
And tell us that it wouldn't rate a line
In Boston or New York,
Vienna, London, Cork,
Would make no delicate cheek incarnadine.

LARRY

We had one of them, but the wheel came off it!
You don't need words that length to tell me straight
Am I dead or am I alive, am I sober or still drunk,
Or why this dizzy, doped, delirious state?

[GRAVEDIGGER *emerges from the room.*]

GRAVEDIGGER

Larry, prepare for the saddest news
That ever your ears have opened to hear;
The shock of your rising levelled your wife,
And she's stretched and dead inside by your bier.

LARRY

Is this the one that was using a knife
To carve me up to save your man's life?

71

TAILORS
It is.

LARRY
Is she the one who couldn't wait
Till the night was out for a second mate?

TAILORS
She is.

LARRY
Is this the one that was willing to wed
The man that had poisoned me, when I was dead?

TAILORS
She is.

LARRY
Is she the wife who said she'd mourn
Till the day that Gabriel blew his horn?
Who said that love should be constant and true
As the mariner's compass or the truest blue?
Who said that the woman who'd marry again
Was ten times worse than a female Cain?

TAILORS
She is.

LARRY
Then to Hell with her!

GRAVEDIGGER
Larry, these are no words
To use of your late respected wife,
She loved and obeyed you for fifteen years
And is one half-minute to cancel a life?

LARRY

One half-minute thrown into that scale
Outweighs all the rest of her life.
She's dead, so God rest her, and God forgive
Her, and every faithless wife.
        I remember her as pleasant
As the little flowers of Spring
With her eyes as brilliant shining
As her ring;
I remember nights together
And evenings in the twilight
When the last threads of radiance
Were not half as fine a sight
As her face, and then the mornings . . .
But all's cancelled, all's erased
And what she is, not what she was
Fills out the future days.

This morning, rising early
There was dew on every grass-blade,
The air thin and clear as music
And Autumn on the way,
The future calm before me,
A friend in every parish,
Youth tamed and love house-broken—
But this was fate's pay-day.
Look at me since this morning,
The dead in droves about me,
My house turned topsyturvy
And funeral bills to pay.

WIDOW

You're no more misfortunate than I,
With my husband dead and his grave not dry,
The land untilled and the thatch unpatched,
The windows open, the door unlatched.

LARRY

Two houses foundered is a woeful case
Is there ne'er a neighbour around the place?

WIDOW

There isn't a soul, and it's lonesome too;
And who is going to manage for you?

LARRY

I'll do well enough once the fuss is done
With a bit of steak or a currany bun.

WIDOW

And the house about you going to rack
And ruin, and not a shirt to your back,
The cups unwashed, the table stained,
The curtains ragged, the cat untrained,
Last week's ashes stuck in the grate,
Your dinner eaten from your breakfast plate.

Oh, well I know the way you'll manage
And soon the neighbours will see the damage,
Getting vexed when they have to be sending
Two or three times for the shoes you're mending,
Their boots sucking water at every puddle,
Heels, soles and teeveens in a miser's muddle,
The heelball missing, the wax-thread flabby,
The old boots wrecked and the new ones shabby,
And before very long you'll see they have found
A cobbler whose soles and heels are sound.

LARRY

I could get a char or a girl by the day.

WIDOW

You know very well what the neighbours would say;
If she was young they'd gossip and gab
And if she was old they'd say that some drab
Slipped in at night when she'd finished her job.
And youthful or old they'd be certain to rob.

LARRY

I might get a young lad from an orphanage
Who'd work for his keep and a very small wage.

WIDOW

Aye, and have him pinching your cigarettes,
Your socks and ties, and making bets
In the village, and the house hanging down in dirt.
No, that's a scheme that never would work.

GRAVEDIGGER

Then what's the poor fellow supposed to do?

SEAMUS

I suppose you want him to marry you!

WIDOW

The less heard from you the better, my boy.
When you're hanging as high as Gilderoy
And the ballad-singers are singing your crime
Then will be your warbling time.
If you've any sense give your throttle no scope
Till you chirp your last song at the end of a rope.

LARRY

I'll have sense from this out to button my mouth
And talk neither of love nor of jealousy
But take every woman as I find her
Expecting and giving no loyalty.
If unsatisfied wives give a curl of the eye
I'll slither at night through their garden gate;
And if innocent girls have a hankering for knowledge
They'll find me an expert if transient mate.
So, husbands beware, young men take a care,
If you see any woman slip into the dark
If I'm not in the room be certain that soon
She'll discover my bite is as bad as my bark.

WIDOW

This is nothing but the wildest talk,
The girls of the parish are safe as a house,
After fifteen years marriage you're never the man
To throw off the traces and go on the loose.

LARRY

I'm a demon if roused and I'll drink and carouse,
I'll court the young girls unbeknown to the law,
I'll have chislers in dozens till there's nothing but cousins
From here to the sea, and they all with one da.

GRAVEDIGGER

Mind, I'm listening and I'll tell the priest
The nasty scheme that's in your head;
Be sure he'll put a stop to that
And put a screen round the marriage bed.

LARRY

Let him put a fence round the island so
For this very night I'll hang out my sign,
"Here young ones! Here's the fellow
That has hotter blood than the best Moonshine!"

GRAVEDIGGER

'Tis a sorry thing when all is said
That your missus raised you from the dead.

WIDOW

Don't mind him at all, this is all old chat
Can't you see in his eye the fun that he's at;
The priest and the peelers can sleep sound at night
While Larry at home will be sleeping as tight.

LARRY

At every pub where the rates aren't paid
And the owner does an all night trade
I'll know the knock, two, three or four
That will bring Jem hurrying out to the door
With voice tuned down and anxious eye
Up the empty street lest the law come by;
Then down the passage and into the snug
Where the light is dim in the cigarette fug,
The half-ones ordered of poisonous stuff
And then the half-jarred garrulous guff

Till the unfamiliar tap at the door
Quenches the light and stills the roar
And cigarettes blooming in the gloom
Are the only signals in the crowded room
And the only noise is the sigh of the drink
As Jem pours the evidence down the sink.
Then maybe the Law will make an entry
Stalking in past the useless sentry,
Notebooks out and deliberate stance
Knowing the alibi in advance,
Making notes of fresh stains of stout
And the simple teetotallers lounging about;
Listening to the touching tale
Of the friendly whiskey, stout and ale
All gratis, and the brandy ready
For the invalid drinker with the heart unsteady,
Hearing how men from three miles away
Happened by chance to pass that way
And drop in for a light for a pipe or a fag—
And the Law with the whole case in the bag
Taking down the fictional name
And the false address from which it came;
The hardy drinkers' alcohol brains
Getting the blood from atrophied veins
Think they're up on a capital charge
And make wild statements to the world at large
Till Jem's unfortunate missus appears
Her hair in pigtails, and in floods of tears
The Law gone into a sort of trance
As she begs on her knees for the one last chance,
"If the licence is endorsed once more
We can take the name from over the door."
While the boozer reckons up in his head
The money spent and the distance to bed,
The chance of a fine and his name in the news
And all for a dose of murdering booze;

And seeing the drooping, blood-shot eye
The blackened nail and the nicotine dye
Reads in advance the next day's log,
The shattered head, the hair of the dog
And knows too well that next Saturday night
Will present his eyes with a similar sight.

WIDOW

I remember my father's dying injunction—
"Drink fusel oil and take extreme unction!"

LARRY

You're as gamey a woman as ever I met
But women are poison I'm starting to think,
And from this day forward I must be content
With a drag on my pipe and a headful of drink.

WIDOW

The pounds of tobacco you stuff in your pipe
May solace a moment, an hour or a day
But when they are smoked you are left with the pipe
And the pleasure and solace are merely heresay;
But a woman that's healthy and loving and young
Gives pleasure for months, or a year, or a life,
When the throat's harsh with smoke she's still sweet
        to the tongue
So who'd chose tobacco in place of a wife?
The drink that's so merry and frisky and gay
So youthful and gallant and brave by lamplight
Is surly and sullen and crazed the next day
And five minutes as long as an hour of the night;
But a woman that's joyous and gamesome and witty
Is as loving at midday as she is at midnight
Her laughter as free and her glances as pretty
In the prose of the day as the verse of starlight.

The drink and the horses, the dogs and the fags
Replenish your interest but empty your pockets,
So cling to a woman in satins or rags
And she'll liven your eyes till they sink in their
    sockets.

LARRY

Your husband told you to hold your horses
Till the clay on his grave was dry
And I think you'd better obey his wish,
And so, I think, should I.

2ND TAILOR

If your Johnny had known, if you had known,
If Larry had known what is to be
This would be a different story
And there would be no me!
But the coroner and jury will find
Death by misadventure
On Herself and the Doctor; and you will marry
Without a word of censure.
The future is calling to us and we
Must fade out of your sight,

[*As he speaks, the other characters on the stage turn to one
another and speak as though the* TAILORS *were no longer
present.*]

Already you've forgotten we're here
So good-luck, and a very good night.

[*The* TAILORS *step to the front of the stage and the inner
curtains are drawn.*]

And so my grandpa married twice,
One wife was good and one was bad;
But which was bad and which was good
Was a puzzle always to my granddad,

For one talked love to him all day long
And the other one did what the world thought
    wrong,
Married in haste and didn't repent,
Laughed at love and was well content
To be faithful and happy, witty and good,
No bitter nagger and no prude,
Well able to drink her bottle of stout
And just as well able to do without,
Her children neat and her home all shining,
Hers was the gold past all refining,
And, son, my wish for you when you marry
Is that you may be as happy as Larry.

[*Curtain*]

APPENDIX: SCENE IIa

The following interlude may be played at the end of Scene II. (Page 38) The new characters are the Three Fates, CLOTHO, LACHESIS *and* ATROPOS.

[*The lights go up and three very old, very decrepit women are sitting on a rock singing. They sing to the traditional Irish Air, 'The Three Lovely Lassies'.*]

THE FATES

We are three old ladies from Hades, Hades, Hades, Hades.
We are three old ladies from Hades,
And we've come like a bird at your call,
And we've come like a bird at your call.

CLOTHO

I'm a spinster whose age is uncertain, uncertain, uncertain, uncertain,
I'm a spinster whose age is uncertain.
But without me you can't rise or fall,
Without me you can't rise or fall.

LACHESIS

I reel thread and weave it and wind it, wind it, wind it, wind it,
I reel thread and weave it and wind it,
My stuff clothes the great and the small,
My stuff clothes the great and the small.

ATROPOS

I snip and I cut and I shorten, shorten, shorten, shorten,
I snip and I cut and I shorten,
So I am the best of them all,
Yes, I am the best of them all.

CLOTHO

Boys, O boys! It's many a year
Since e'er a Tailor called our name.
Working we've been, ignored, abused,
Unpaid, unpraised, a walking shame.

LACHESIS

But for the scarlet silken thread
We spin and weave and gently cut
No birth or life or death could be,
The shop of life, unstocked, might shut.

ATROPOS

We're tied and old and spent and lean
Our fingers worn, our eyes near lost,
Our youth forgotten, our beauty spoiled,
All roads we take are lined with frost.

LACHESIS

But you six lads have brought us here,
Reminded us of days in Greece,
When honour was where honour shone
And none insulted Lachesis,

CLOTHO

Or Atropos or Clotho scorned;
So tell us what you want to do;
Pumpkin will turn to golden coach,
And queens will sigh at night for you.

ATROPOS

Your yarn will turn to cloth of gold,
Your stout be endless, full your purse,
Armies will sing behind you or
Nations will wither at your curse.

LACHESIS

Happy in silk you'll sprawl all day
Beguiled by troops of nubile girls,
Or, drunk as Bacchus you may lie
Being gently pelted with large pearls.

ATROPOS

All tickets that you buy will win
You fifty thousand in the Sweep;
A moderate sun will keep you tanned
From New Year's Day till Christmas Week.

LACHESIS

All gifts that Tailors might have asked
And disremembered will be yours;
Name anything the heart can prize
From cigarettes to Koh-i-noors.

SECOND TAILOR

What we had in mind was smaller
And wouldn't be much trouble;
I know that you three ladies
Could lay Dublin town in rubble,
But what my friends and I want
Is a passport to the ages
To rectify a story
And assure our heritages.

ATROPOS

What is time, child? It's a toy,
A top to spin, a clock to wind;
Set it where you will and soon
You'll know that time is in your mind.
We're old and tired, but thought is free
And thought can make us young again.

[*There is a peal of thunder and a blackout, during which the* FATES *throw off their ancient masks and cloaks and appear when the lights go up young and radiant.*]

 Make thought your stallion and he'll leap
 To any year the heart can name.

[*They sing, to the tune of 'Three Lovely Lasses', but now in swing-time.*]

THE FATES

We are three young ladies from Hades, Hades,
 Hades,
We are three young ladies from Hades
And we're ready for kisses and love,
And we're ready for kisses and love.

CLOTHO

I'm a spinster, but ready for marriage, marriage,
 marriage,
I'm a spinster, but ready for marriage,
So who'll take me on as his bride?
So who'll take me on as his bride?

LACHESIS

And I'll make my lover immortal, immortal,
 immortal,
And I'll make my lover immortal
If he'll kiss me and call me his own.
If he'll kiss me and call me his own.

ATROPOS

At heart I'm a simple young maiden, maiden,
 maiden,
At heart I'm a simple young maiden,
Though they call me a Fate worse than Death,
Though they call me a Fate worse than Death.

FOURTH TAILOR

Well! Imagine these three young ones
Being in charge of all creation,
Controlling the elections
And every complication
Of living and of dying
And of, even, incubation;
No wonder that we see such signs
Of the times' degeneration.

FIRST TAILOR

In meeting ladies of this class
You should show your education
By shutting up and leaving talk
To those men whose vocation
Is oratory and rhetoric
And constant emulation
Of the eloquence that in the Dail
Bedazzles the whole nation.

SIXTH TAILOR

That's all damn fine, but what's the price
For meddling with the Universe?
I never knew a woman yet
Gave anything free—except a curse.

ATROPOS

We want to be loved
And we want to be kissed
We want to know all
That so far we have missed,
Will you dance, will you kiss,
Will you clasp, will you couple,
And all that you ask will be paid on the double.

CLOTHO

We are greater than gods,
We are older than time,
But our hearts are still young,
They are still at their prime.
Will you dance, will you kiss,
Will you clasp, will you couple,
And all that you ask will be paid on the double.

LACHESIS

We have sat by the shore
Of infinity's lake
And dreamt of the lovers
That some day we'd take.
Will you dance, will you kiss,
Will you clasp, will you couple,
And all that you ask will be paid on the double.

ATROPOS

We are women, and women
Need loving, need pressing,
Soft words and soft music,
Sweet lies and caressing.
Will you dance, will you kiss,
Will you clasp, will you couple,
And all that you ask will be paid on the double.

CLOTHO

We're omniscient, omnipotent,
Omniform, omnipresent,
But in matters of love
We are still juvenescent.
Will you dance, will you kiss,
Will you clasp, will you couple,
And all that you ask will be paid on the double.

LACHESIS

So make us your pupils
And teach us to love,
We'll have kisses for keepsakes
That none can remove.
Will you dance, will you kiss,
Will you clasp, will you couple,
And all that you ask will be paid on the double.

[*As they speak they make love in mime to the* TAILORS *who are obviously terrified of the amorous* FATES. *Then* LACHESIS *shows a spindle, while* CLOTHO *and* ATROPOS *hold a long scarlet thread.* ATROPOS *also holds a large scissors.*]

LACHESIS

All years are here, I turn this round
And past is future, future past;
What is to be, or is, or was
The last is first and first is last.

[*The lights begin to flicker as she turns the spindle. There is the sound of rushing wind. The* TAILORS *huddle together down left.*]

Say now what year or place or hour
You would be stopped at, time is free,
Backward and forward spins the wheel,
Choose day or hour in history.

[*There is a whistling sound and the rushing of wind through which the* TAILORS' *voices can be heard.*]

TAILORS [*variously*]

Eh, stop the bus, we can't get off.
Give us a look. Who's that down there?
Where are we going? Oh, the heat.
Janey, we're flying through the air.

LACHESIS

What year, what month, what day, what hour
Of all time passing, past, to come
Is your desire now? Make your choice
And time will stop its pendulum.

FOURTH TAILOR

Bad cess to you! Stop your Andrew Martins;
I'm half-pralatic. There goes me hat.
Will you stop your wheel of fortune turning
Before the six of us are knocked flat.

THIRD TAILOR

There's a whirl and whirling, a skirl and skirling,
A roaring wind, a windy roar,
Our eyes are dazzled with light or lightning,
What was behind us is now before.

LACHESIS

Make your choice, all time lies spread
Before you like a coloured map;
Plan your course now, say what hour
Encompassed your grandpapa's mishap.

SECOND TAILOR

The rush of the years as they fly by
Has dazzled, bewildered, dazed my head.
How can I say what hour is which
As centuries flash by overhead
And at my feet are centuries,
Men born, unborn and men long dead?
Will you stop, will you wait, will you give us a
    chance
To find the warp for the woof of your thread?
[LACHESIS *ceases to turn her spindle. The lights stop
flickering; the noises die down. The* TAILORS *regain their
balance.*]

LACHESIS

Return then to the prison cell
That keeps you bound within one day;
Free as the stars you saw all time
With eyes too weak to watch the play.

FOURTH TAILOR [*running forward to the* FATES]

Whatever cod-acting is going on here
There's one thing is certain—I'm off like a flash:
Whoever you are, you bold-looking things,
Count me out when you bring the world down
    with a crash.
[*To the other* TAILORS]
A halter of snow would lead some that I know
To meddling with history, religion and laws,
But I'll stick to my beads and I'll tell Father Pat
The way that his parish is led by the nose.
[*He proceeds to the exit, but is stopped by the voice of*
ATROPOS.]

ATROPOS

Little man, you are nothing, a seed that is sown,
The flower of a morning, a match in the night,
A speck on the sand of infinity's shore.
One snip and you're gone . . .
[*She prepares to cut.*]

FOURTH TAILOR

Eh, Missus. Hold tight.
[*He comes back.*]

ATROPOS

My scissors are powerful. My vision is bright;
I can see at this moment the spot to alight.
So goodbye now, goodbye, take off for the past.
One snip and you're gone . . .

[*The* FATES *are by now seated again on the rock, which is now pulled off the stage carrying them out of sight. A backcloth of gauze is dropped and the cut-out frame of the scene is taken away and the scene changes quickly to the outside of Larry's house.*]

The play Resumes at page 39.

8.—LEG-BAIL: To take leg-bail is to escape from custody, probably from the idea of the leg receiving bail.

cf. 'It grieved my heart to see you sail
Huroo! Huroo!
It grieved my heart to see you sail
Though from my heart you took leg-bail,
Like a cod you're doubled up head and tail,
Och, Johnny I hardly knew ye!' (*Old Ballad*).

11.—ACT: Almost any human action may be referred to, generally satirically or humourously, as an Act, frequently prefaced by the adjectives 'gas' or 'extraordinary.'

11.—GAS: adj. Amusing, funny, queer.
n. Fun, amusement.

12.—OULD ONES: Old women. The word 'one' is used in a slightly offensive sense of a woman of any age.

12.—JEM.—Jem is the generic Dubliner. The use of the name is typical of the inveterate Irish reluctance to make a positive statement, since it can substitute for any name, known or unknown. cf. also 'your man' q.v.

12.—HOOSH: To give a leg up, to lift.

13.—BOLD.—A slightly satiric adjective. Generally pronounced 'bould.'

13.—FAIR ENOUGH: Very well. This is a cant-phrase of half-humourous acceptance which has achieved vast popularity in recent years.

13.—BALL OF MALT: A glass of whiskey. The word Ball is a corruption of 'Boll,' a measure of capacity for grain.

18.—A FINE FIRE WHEN IT STARTS: The fox at the time was observing steam rising from a heap of stones, and, misled by the proverb, thought there could be no smoke without fire.

20.—KNOCKING BACK: Drinking. The phrase is used particularly in reference to pints of porter—"Knocking back a pint."

29.—SLOUTHERING: Ingratiating, flattering.

34.—A PIPE AND GLASS: This refers to the old custom at wakes of providing the mourners with drink, generally porter, and clay-pipes and tobacco. In addition snuff was provided in large quantities and passed frequently from hand to hand, each recipient being expected to say a prayer for the repose of the soul of the deceased at each sniff taken. Hence the proverbial expression, "Tossed about like snuff at a wake."

46.—MOIDERED: Deafened and confused by excessive noise (also moithered, moythered).

47.—BOWSEY: A low and truculent person. Probably from German *böse,* angry, unpleasant, the word being introduced by the German troops of William III at the end of the 17th century.

57.—BLUESTONE POTEEN: Harried manufacturers of illicit spirits, known as poteen, frequently become impatient at the desultory 'working' of the contents of their still and insert a quantity of Bluestone, or sulphate of copper, to precipitate the action, with lamentable effects on their subsequent customers.

57.—RED BIDDY: In England a comparatively innocuous cheap red wine. In Ireland an almost lethal dose of cheap red wine liberally laced with methylated spirits.

57.—JOHNNY JUMP-UP: A particularly potent cider.

57.—AS DRY AS ST. PATRICK'S DAY: In Ireland St. Patrick's Day is one of mourning to serious drinkers since all public bars, with the exception of that at a phenomenally successful Dog Show in Dublin, are closed.

61.—POOR LARRY: With exquisite illogicality one who has inherited the wealth of eternity is referred to as poor.

69.—PLAIN: Draught single X porter, still retailing, despite the rise in the cost of living, at eightpence a pint, but no longer, as we are assured it did in Edwardian times, sticking to the counter.

69.—LUNATIC SOUP: A very strong cider, possibly with an admixture of other drink, popular with the Army.

69.—MOUNTJOY: The chief Dublin prison and scene of the demise of Irish murderers.

69.—THAT ONE'S STEEL: A cant phrase, mainly among adolescents intent on impressing each other with their prowess. The words are spoken while exhibiting a grimy fist under the nose of an antagonist—"That's iron, that's steel, and here's the one that'll make you squeal!" The third fist being, of course, the first one, is re-exhibited.

70.—LORRY HIM UP: The full phrase is, "Lorry him up, he's no relation." "Lorry" is from Irish *liuradh*, a thrashing. (There is also a faint possibility that it dates from the Anglo-Irish and Civil Wars when troublesome political figures were hustled into a lorry and removed to an 'unknown destination' from which they seldom returned).

70.—H.O.H.A.: When a fight is imminent, a warning cry of "H.O.H.A. Hit one hit all!" may be raised, thereby making it clear that if one of a party is struck every man of the party will consider himself assaulted.

70.—YOUR MAN: May refer to any person living or dead and provides a convenient manner of speaking in riddles.

71.—WE HAD ONE OF THEM, BUT THE WHEEL CAME OFF IT: A satiric reply to any long and cumbersome word or sentence.

75.—TEEVEEN: A side patch on a boot (Ir. *Taoibhín*).

76.—AS HIGH AS GILDEROY, also "As high as Gilderoy's kite," a proverbial expression for great height. Gilderoy, hanged in Edinburgh in the reign of Queen Mary, met his death on a gallows so high that he is said to have looked to the populace like a kite.

76.—CHISLERS: Children. Corruption of the old plural of child, *childer*.

77.—HERE YOUNG ONES: The full phrase is "Young ones! here's young fellas!" It is the courting cry of the adolescent, an invitation to the opposite sex which may, of course, be varied to "Young fellas! here's young ones!"

77.—SNUG: A small enclosed space inside the door of old-fashioned public houses where ladies who *are* ladies may have a drink without enduring the rude stares of men. Also the primitive precursor of the modern lounge, a dingy back-room decorated with spitoons.

77.—HALF-ONE: Half a glass of Irish whiskey. Also a Small One and "Will you do the needful there, Jem!"

77.—HALF-JARRED: Half drunk. A *Jar* is a drink of any kind and *Jarred* is drunk.

77.—GUFF: Talk, generally senseless and sometimes truculent. (Ir. *guth*, a voice).

80.—HERSELF: Generally means the Woman of the House. Used by a husband of a wife, by a servant of a mistress. Similarly *Himself* means The Boss.